ASPIRATION

ASPIRATION

GEORGE ALBON

OMNIDAWN PUBLISHING
RICHMOND, CALIFORNIA
2013

Cover art: *Prop*, Elspeth Pratt, 2010
baltic birch, plywood
83" x 93" x 16" approx.
Photo: Toni Hafkenscheid, courtesy of Diaz Contemporary, Toronto

Cover and Interior Design by Peter Burghardt

Typefaces: Cambria and Futura Medium

Printed on Glatfelter Natures Natural 50# Archival Quality Recycled Paper

Cataloguing-in-Publication Data is available from the Library of Congress

Published by Omnidawn Publishing, Richmond, California
www.omnidawn.com   (510) 237-5472   (800) 792-4957
10 9 8 7 6 5 4 3 2 1
ISBN: 978-1-890650-85-8

Aspiration is the first part of a four-part section about the lyric, to be followed by *Practice*, *Immanence*, and *Migration*. This four-part section in its turn is one of the ten sections of a work-in-progress called *Café Multiple*.

In Don DeLillo's *Ratner's Star,* a group of crack mathematical theoreticians have convened to make sense of a series of radio pulses from that eponymous, distant star, pulses that might be an attempt at communication from extraterrestrials. A hundred pages in, they take a break from their brain labor to watch a reputed genuine levitation. A flat-cart is wheeled into a room. A body-sized cowl, and a presumed occupant beneath it, are atop the cart. Under the cowl sits a cross-legged holy man, unviewable through the material, but whose authenticity is vouchsafed to the assembled mathematicians by the holy man's guardian. The latter's introductory remarks, growing more smoke-and-mirrors with every sentence, drive most of the assembled out before he's even concluded them. But the dozen who remain witness something. After a dramatic pause the form beneath the cowl begins to turn axially inside it. The cowl itself doesn't turn but registers the motions of its interior occupant, who is steadily gaining velocity, like a top getting faster rather than slower with each revolution. At a critical cross-over between drag and lift the figure hovers up from its seat a few inches, spinning like nobody's business. Then the cowl snaps in mid-air and settles back onto the cart, an empty wrap. The holy man has vanished. He has perhaps managed to dematerialize himself and reconstitute his essence as a frequency set that can communicate with the pulses. The mathies don't know what to make of it. Then a handwritten note starts to circulate among them.

> *It's done with an isometric graviton axis.*
> *I saw it twice in a nightclub act in Perth.*
> *Pass it on.*

It's familiar DeLillo location, with its gizmo of other-temptation taking up psychic room amid rationality's minions. And yet they all crowded in to have a look.

DeLillo has an interesting shade in his books, inside of which sophisticated individuals, people whose self-worth involves not having anything put over on them—the caste who "know the levels"—also constitute a demographic of closet seekers, invested in ideas of the withheld and the occluded, "some deeply saving force," meaningfully unknown *and indivisible by sophistication,* a something beyond that, were the conduction pitched in the right way, would give them permission to drop their defenses and live with less quantifiable inclusions.

This scene with the cowl has come back to me lately, as I've fidgeted over the shape and matter of a stretch of writing that would touch issues inside and around the modern lyric. Most of the fidgeting has been pure reluctance. Reluctance to give myself over to a thing, a chimerical energy, that relates more familiarly to disparation and radical combination and atopic crossings and weightless magnification and submerged affiliations, only to entangle myself trying to isolate some of that energy with the kind of verbal mass that falls into sentences. To presume parity with something hidden and spinning. And to imagine that I can get away with letting that thing in motion spiral out to four curving paths or infills, with near-arbitrary designations— *aspiration, practice, immanence,* and *migration*—without betraying the cowl, the skin without inscription, that gives three-dimensionality to belief and commitment.

> *Once again a book of Henry Corbin's arrives uncannily to comment on a maze of explanation! After "belief and commitment," I shut down the laptop to take a break and continue where I left off in "Creative Imagination in the Sūfism of Ibn ʿArabī." Getting to the first footnote of the afternoon (never a long wait in Corbin), I turned to the back and read it. Commenting on a verse from*

the Koran (L: 14) which chides certain of the pious who won't accept a renewed vision of the forms of beings, when first creation produced no such reluctance, Corbin writes: "The Arabic term translated by 'doubt' signifies both confusion, ambiguity (labs) and to put on a garment (lubs)." This dual etymology folds together and energizes a shared space of the hidden and the newly-revealed: "Thus beneath the exoteric (standardized) translation of the verse there appears the theological meaning of Ibn ʿArabī.: 'Should we be powerless to clothe them in a new creation?'"

While the math-folk are still seated, wondering whether or not the show is over, a man of indeterminate age, though old enough to have prominent pouches under his eyes ("an elderly twelve-year-old," someone says to his neighbor), begs their indulgence for a few minutes more. He passes out a photocopied document to each of them. His captives roll or blanch their eyes as they thumb-check the number of pages and look at the solid continuous block of text they are being (asked?) (told?) to read. Shifting sounds: haunches on leatherette, squeaks of folding chairs during changes of position. At different rates and levels of interest, and strangely conscious of the tiniest ambient noise around and outside the room (places they could be instead of here), each begins to at least scan the document's contents.

> *The lyric is emergent—gestural or suggestive—rather than substantive or complete. The lyric is an urge towards the future based upon an appetite in the present. The lyric is an intermediate world that shows itself fugitively, as an opening of shutters that immediately close up, and makes itself felt as a dimension of being surprised, a disturbance, a fissure, an obstacle, a stumbling upon that reveals a beyond, and by which the subject feels overwhelmed. The lyric seems to offer a powerful condensation of emotional and identity linkages—specifically, a certain interface between abjection and defiance. The lyric incorporates antagonistic perspectives without explaining any of them away, and also without reconciling them in a spurious sublation or higher unity. The lyric is both a fresh creation of spacetime and an immediate perishing. The lyric is an ecological production of actual togetherness, where ecological means that the aim is not toward a unity beyond differences, which would reduce those differences through a goodwill reference to abstract*

principles of togetherness, but toward a creation of concrete, interlocked, asymmetrical, and always partial graspings. The lyric is the thunderbolt observed about the attraction of amber and the Heraclean stones. The lyric struggles actively with the given <u>bodily</u> code for material accumulation until it surrenders, as well, some of its immemorial meanings of the accumulation of spiritual, physical, sexual, and intellectual power. The lyric is a process whereby individuation creates a relational system that holds together what prior to its occurrence was incompatible. Alongside the connective synthesis of flows and cuts, the lyric is a disjunctive synthesis of routes and permutations. The economy of production is supplemented in the lyric by an economy of circulation and distribution. This supplemental economy corresponds to a torsion in the field of desiring production. The lyric is a schizophrenic clattering. The lyric becomes ranges not determinants. It cannot be presented directly, or re-presented; but its very indeterminacy is a perfectly positive, objective structure which acts as a focus or horizon within perception. The lyric is a relatedness backward or forward. The lyric is a flight to valuable qualities. The lyric is the emanation *of something that makes itself known but conceals itself in the appearance. The lyric offers itself to be felt by other entities in its own turn, so that it is referent beyond itself. What is peculiar to the lyric is the fact that questioning becomes lucid in advance. The lyric does not prefigure the actualities that emerge from it. Rather, it is the impelling force, or the principle, that allows each actual entity to appear (to manifest itself) as something new, something without precedence or resemblance, something that has never existed in the universe in quite that way before. The lyric converts its exclusions into contrasts. The lyric is not "observed," it is there in a heedful adjustment. Looking forward, the lyric induces the process of actualization; looking backward, it is an expression of that process. The lyric is the exploring, playful, transgressive forcing of routine practices away from their structure, as a possible preliminary to the establishment of new automatic concatenations (at which point "the lyric" will already be somewhere else, forcing the new structure away from itself). The lyric is always somehow directed and underway. The lyric is the constant onrush of the road, the simultaneous recession of new reaches of dark pavement illumined by the onrushing headlights, the sense of the turnpike itself as something enormous, abandoned, and derelict. The lyric is a tit-for-tat intercourse between two hands. The lyric is the reserve force of information, the reservoir of presumptive, deniable, and unarticulated knowledge, that images itself also as a reservoir of ever-violable innocence. The lyric is a queer but long-married young woman whose erotic and intellectual life is fiercely intransitive. In the lyric thought is stimulated, rather than paralyzed, when it is pushed to its limit. The lyric's autopoietic final causality also works to reproduce sameness and avert fundamental change. The lyric is not exhausted by the event into which it ingresses, or which includes it; it never loses its accent of potentiality. It remains available for other events, other actualizations. The lyric is a vector feeling, that is to say, feeling from a beyond which is to be determined. The lyric must acknowledge its perpetual growth, which is a quality awkward and vital. The lyric is a state of tension, or contradiction, full of potential energy that, given the right sort of push, will be discharged, causing a transformation. In the lyric, every new necessarily provides its own negations; but negativity is not in any*

sense the lyric's inner principle. The lyric may become
explicitly accessible as such for the first time when we do
not find something in its place.

No, DeLillo does not give this printout to his math-characters, and no, none of these definitions, poached by me from a variety of sources, has *the lyric* as its original referent. As the voice in the car alarm says, they have been tampered with. On the other hand, some of them, in their jammed manipulations, end up inventing things about the lyric that make me pause. The last one in particular will have touched anyone with whom poetry engages as a volumetric both having and lacking volumes, as a movement that expands upon occupation. A koan involving void, drift, and claim, it suggests prenominal appearance, but from a place with sufficient gravitational pull—call it history?— to have established the practice of searching there.

And here there is another scene, in another room, where like-minded folk also confront a singularity. This was John Cage's "Empty Words" lecture at the Naropa Institute in 1974, a two and a half hour presentation consisting of Cage's pronouncing an arrangement of sounds excavated from words in H. D. Thoreau's journal, with some of its drawings projected overhead. After half an hour, the large audience lost "attendance." They started behaving like the twelve-year-olds in *The 400 Blows* when the teacher faced away to write something on the blackboard. (Cage read his text with his back to them.) They whooped, they whistled, they made farting noises. Cage held his ground, took his time and didn't stop until the piece was completed. When he finally faced his audience, he was stern. By turning away I wasn't giving you permission to act like morons, he told them. I was giving you a space in which to be mindful. When one of them asked, why draw a line, he responded, "it's the line that I've drawn, and to which my life is devoted."

I myself would have loved hearing vowel and consonant sounds —phonemes and silence—proceed through a performance, and would have stayed to the end. But I would have become restive at about the same time that the interruptions began. And isn't it possible that several in the audience may have already drawn their lines and were devoting their lives to liberating words in their own way? Cage's kind of ritual theater, its challenging expanding power, plays best if the requirement of ritual deportment is clear. Otherwise the audience, in chairs that face one way toward a frontal event, may be at something that feels to them like a mix of concert and lecture, and not happily attuning to either. (His written directions have the speaker facing the audience and only later turning his back, and not to separate himself but to share the same perspective.) My own imagination would place it outdoors, in a grove, say, with only a few listening participants, while Cage or someone else carefully sounded the work in concert with twig-movement and messages of birds and insects. Then the *aspiration,* the word for this first movement, might rise from the ground and become one of the drifts to claim, most suffusive just at the point of evaporation.

It can be pronounced open-mouthed, with one hitch. The stop is the *p,* a lodged object, which forces closure and stops the hum. That this word means hope and even a sort of ardor is the reason for crowning my text with it, but there's a paradox too, since pronunciatory aspiration is about sounding consonants. This is as it should be. If vowels are the sky-path, consonants are rock shapes seen up close. But as I pull back to an imagined beginning, the shapes vaporize, and before long I am left with what new life might hear inside itself as *the sound,* an originating appeal, the primordial esophageal vibration, the deep entrance. The open sounds open, infant appeal is that territory.

The ah shape of the mouth, prior to articulation

A sound that is toward something but is also the thing itself

The ah shape of the mouth, articulation in its pure state

Ah the speech of the body before the mind knows syntax. An ah during massage, during pain, during love, is the body apart, left to its sound. It is whole and hole, the thing next to nothing, a tenacious mortal grip.

Allen Ginsberg loved his ahs. Ah, sunflower, weary of time, he heard Blake say to him in the rented room. In a few years he told a fellow inmate at Rockland State Hospital, ah, Carl, while you are not safe I am not safe. A few years after that, in Berkeley and thinking of Whitman, ah, dear father, graybeard, lonely old courage-teacher. His *om* through a microphone in Chicago's Grant Park during the 1968 Democratic Convention was an ah meant to calm the crowds and dissipate negative energy. Years later, a celebrity on a talk show, he explained that chanting the Hare Krishna mantra produced an after-effect similar to the post-coital Sigh, which he demonstrated with impressive attenuation. With minutes left to live, he woke from his coma and looked around the room, at the suddenly startled onlookers—the gathered friends and lovers, the Buddhist monks—and uttered one final ah before joining eternity.

The Mithraic invocation, part of a theurgic rite with remarkable powers of tenacity, was practiced in one form or another two hundred years after the birth of the Nazarene. In this Mystery, a candidate for the higher gnosis convened with the brethren whose peer he aspired to be. Like other cultic initiatory rites, this one was secret, "recessed," it took place in a cave. The initiate was required to recite a lengthy entreaty composed of nine "utterances" the centerpiece of which was a procession of "root sounds," expressions of the elementariness of a raw soul. It consisted entirely of vowels. An initiate's attempt to give voice to his soul-nature would have been the pivotal moment in life. If he communicated forcefully, the brethren might commence an "awe reaction" of poppings, hissings, and plosives involving lip, tongue, tooth, and roof of mouth— responses at the "gate" in antiphony with the initiate's diaphragmatic processing of vowels. The cave was then the right place. It was not only appropriately occluded as befits hermetic practice, but emblematic of that cavern inside the soul-animal where the vibration is gathered before massing it into sonorities that meet the atmosphere just outside the intoning flesh,

ëeö • oëeö • iöö • oë • ëeö • ëeö • oëeö • iöö • oëëe • öëe • öoë • ië • ëö • oö • oë • ieö • oë • öoë • ieöoë • ieeö • eë • iö • oë • ioë • öëö • eoë • oeö • öië • öiëeö • oi • iii • ëoë • öuë • ëö • oëe • eöëia • aëaeëa • ëeeë • eeë • eeë • ieö • ëeö • oëeeoë • ëeö • euö • oë • eiö • ëö • öë • öë • öë • ee • ooouiöë!

Ah to uh: the pull downward, the pressure shift. Lust getting its proper vowel:

Frank O'Hara, for whom every poem was truly new, breaks off a large prose block in "Day and Night in 1952" and spins out 33 lines ending with *of*. "...you of/ the paper route, you fictitious of/ all the prancers in my ardent imagination of/ which you are not the least and most of/ what I think about the world of/ no illusion, not an iota! Not hated of..." Add an ell and you have love, but lop off the eff and you have *uh,* more compelling, more circumstantial. It's the ardent body requiring continuances, further conveyances. Steady moans. An "excitement-prone" poet revving an imaginary gas pedal 33 times, on his way from Midtown to a Hampton or coming back from a weekend or leaving for one. The scutch of dancers' feet tromping through an "airy" section involving the entire company, as heard from a seat too close to the stage. His acutely judging intelligence was nevertheless eager to make room for this kind of pleasing surfeit, just as the era's cultural operations happily admitted it into the prevailing discursiveness. (There is also the word's simple-tool meaning, its accordion expansions.)

When the monk asked Master Joshu, does a dog have Buddha-nature, the Master replied: MU. Mu means no, but the Master wasn't giving a negative reply to the monk's question. He was saying MU. He wasn't saying it. He was bellowing it, the way the gathered sound of the world might. Annihilating either/or. Negation to scour the mind of dualities. Sounding from the mouth by necessity, the gut trying to meet the throat. One consonant, one vowel, bottom-deep, an intense performative roar. The student must burn with MU. Unswallowable, unvomitable, a red-hot iron ball lodged in the throat. The body charged to work the mind through to a non-discriminating state. The Master's reply was better—that is, more challenging— than silence, another possible reply to initiates. Better, because silence is a recasting of the either/or, even a form of "the literary." Rinzai Zen, working with koans, asks for performative responses, which partake of the both/and indispensable to enlightenment. And, complementary to zazen sitting practice, they inform the body. Like a typo I once made and then kept in a notebook because it seemed usable, *MU* is *oractice*. At the sanzen, the appointment between student and teacher, the former will try to deliver the most earth-shaking *MU* possible, while the latter will listen and gauge the quality of practice— what is good, what needs work, how the sitting posture might be improved. The teacher's response might be his own *MU,* as Shodo Harada Roshi demonstrated to a student in a filmed sanzen at the Sogen-ji monastery in Okayama. The student, a husky bear of a man, let loose with a truly fearsome sound, followed by silence as Harada Roshi sifted what he had heard. Then, working his mouth slightly and gathering something up, this Gandhi-sized man erupted with a *MU* not only louder but at least a half octave lower than his charge, who took it inside and then skittered from the sanzen room.

Spirit invoked in Sūfism is inspirit, breath entering, escaping. Louis Massignon describes "two sharply contrasting words, *nafs* and *rūḥ*. *Nafs* is the breath of the throat: it comes from the entrails, it is "carnal" and bound up with the blood, it causes eructation and spitting and confers the enjoyment of flavor. *Rūḥ* is the breath of the nostrils: it comes from the brain, it causes nasal speech and sneezing, it confers the sense of smell and the discernment of spiritual qualities." Henry Corbin, in another context: "The specific center of love is in Sūfism generally held to be the *rūḥ, pneuma,* spirit,"—a more vital center, even, than the heart. *Rūḥ,* the breath of life, is also a restless, inquisitive wind. It doesn't die when the body does but slips away, a wanderer.

Nafs and *rūḥ* permeate the Sūfi universe. *Nafs,* the breath of the throat, is "soul" in counterpart with the "spirit" of the *rūḥ,* but there are also complexes like the *Nafas al-Raḥmān,* the Sigh of Compassion, uttered by Allah—"the Sad One"—in isolation, out of sympathy and out of the need of sympathy, the need of something else to share feeling with. Corbin's generative understanding of breath-of-spirit enables him to describe this Sigh with distinct stresses each time. It is variously a Breath of the existentiating divine Compassion, the Compassionate Sigh, an Effusion of Being, the Breath exhaled by the Sadness of the Pathetic God, the Sigh that actualizes the reality of the "thou."

Rūḥ is a sinuous pneumatic valence in everyday life and localities, it is part of the working of things. It is a good ghost making its rounds, offering unseen but fully apprehended aid to those who know how to respect and use it. In the vestigial Moroccan society Stefania Pandolfo studied, the *rûḥ* (spelled with her preferred diacritic) is the thing that comes into the weaving spaces and binds the work, as the Maghribî weavers ply the bamboo sticks that control the warp and weft, and thus "the intersection that is weaving," and which operate "the *rûḥ* of the loom—its life breath. For in weaving the *rûḥ* does not pre-exist its 'capturing': it is produced by it. What is generated and delivered by women through a series of ritualized technical steps is the loom as an articulated body, as an alive being: a creature with *rûḥ*." A conspiring of hand and spirit surely inseparable from the breath of the faithful, and their phonic modes of worship.

In some Koranic recitation, the words are spoken with a performative deliberation that shifts the relation between speech and meaning, between hearing and understanding. "Muslims made every effort to learn by heart the sacred text of the Koran," Massignon writes, "which they had heard and read, combining the two breaths *nafs* and *rūḥ* to produce the rhythm of their recitation: vocalizing and nasalizing (*rūḥ*) the consonants (*nafs,* which alone are noted in the manuscripts) in a staccato manner, thus designedly polarizing the ambivalent three-letter roots. They hoped to recapture the initial divine breath which had first dictated the sacred text by means of this insinuating, persuasive collective declamation which pierces to the heart." This is recitation as re-creation. The Words of God were first heard in rudiments, they were heard in sequences of pause and isolate pronouncing. As reconstituted in the sound of the faithful, recitation casts the material-verbal into an auditopia wherein it is cyclically broken down and newly created. Not a violence performed on the Words, but worshipful accentuation of their originating particulate forces. Vowels, consonants, intensities of utterance. Not back to zero but back to the start—saying the grains.

Hugo Ball delivered his *Verse ohne Worte,* poems without words, before an audience in the Cabaret Voltaire, on June 23, 1916. In the middle of his performance he found himself riding his syllables to church. Through the smoke-choked confines of the Cabaret, his recitation gained in volumes and rhythms, as he realized that these sound poems could either sink back into novelty or cross a threshold into apotropaic incantation jolifanto bambla　o　falli　bambla. It was a conscious decision but so is the one to jump across a widening chasm if you're on the part sinking into the cataclysm. The cataclysm surrounding them all was the unspeakable First World War and its complacently participating societies. "Our cabaret is a gesture," Ball had said. "Every word that is spoken and sung here says at least one thing: that this humiliating age has not succeeded in winning our respect." Ball had made a costume in which, from which, to deliver his poems grossiga m'pfa habla horem. His legs were enclosed in shiny blue cardboard, his trunk in a single large cylinder. Around his shoulders was a large cardboard collar flaring stiffly past his elbows. His hat was another cylinder, and more cardboard, striped blue and white. Paper claws reached out past his fingers. The whole thing rendered him unable to walk or clutch, he had to be carried on before the recitation and off afterward, "like a magical bishop." Or, it might seem, like a fetish object, a shamanic radio console, a mechanical fortuneteller in a glass box. Hugo Ball shifted from side to side, heavily sweating, and intoned the *Verse ohne Worte,* spread out on multiple music stands. bosso fataka

ü   üü   ü

schampa wulla   wussa   olobo

In a value-destroyed world, a world of bankers' venality, this Dadaist's first hope was to take the damage and make it explicit.

Inside his radical spirit-house the phonemes were called up, ravished, and summarily re-ordered—a gauntlet thrown down at European obtuseness. In destruction was reclamation. A poem without words is still a poem, with a poem's wobbly uncatchable powers. Ball's "deliverance" that night was his last performance at the Cabaret, which would itself soon close. The Voltaire's pressurized mix of entertainment and prophecy was an acute intervention; continuance past that phase would have turned it into entertainment and any other place. In his journal a year later he wonders if "perhaps the art which we are seeking is the key to every former art: a salomonic key that will open all mysteries." Hugo Ball was serious about tending the world. After the Cabaret he worked in the Swiss capital doing diplomacy and leftist journalism, before his final years as a devout Catholic living in the Italian canton of the Swiss Alps. The townspeople soon realized they had a special person in their midst, and not from anything they'd read but from encounters with his guileless, franciscan temperament. They sought his counsel on matters great and small. He died there in 1927, a man with an interesting past, venerated by a local population who had shared his presence long after the Syllables had been broken and started over.

Elsewhere, an "Oriental" Russian named Velimir Khlebnikov descended the cliff face of his own language to get down to its alphabet, and then descended underground to the sounds, the humus out of which meanings break open and germinate. "With м begin names signifying the very smallest members of several sets of things." Moss midge mite minnow moth. (Some work in English.) There is also *zerna maka,* poppy seed, and *mizinets,* the little finger. And *mig,* instant. His idealism mixed philology with earth physics; in his "alphabet of the mind" each Cyrillic letter looked and spoke in such a way as to throw its own dynamic away from itself and join the causative behaviors of the world. One letter is *a movement born of a difference in pressures.* Another is *the transposition of an element from one field force to another.* And "ж [*zh*] is the freedom to move independently of one's neighbors. From which we get *zhidkii* [liquid, watery], and *zhivoi* [alive, lively], and everything near the water—*zhabry* [gills], *zhaba* [a toad], *zhazhda* [thirst], *zhalga* [a water-weed]. In *zh* we have the separation of the dry principle, full of movement, from water, the struggle between fire and water. In the opinion of the ancients there was an equals sign drawn between water and time (past). Whence the kinship between *zhazhdat* [thirst] and *zhdat'* [wait]. *Zh* is frequently the separation of water from the fiery element."

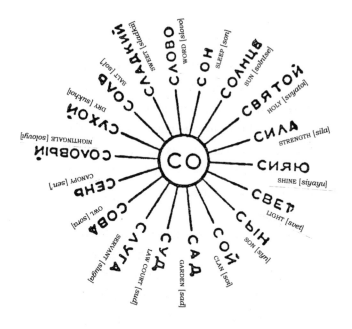

Taking the Russian word **co** ("with" in English, and heard syllabically as *so*), he positions it as a seed-center with radiating petals, and notices correspondences, natural attachments—words engendered from **co**, or of primordial relation. This field from a single seed-word is populated by, among others, *son*

[sleep], *solntse* [sun], *sila* [strength], *slovo* [word], *syn* [son], *sol'* [salt], *sova* [owl], *soi* [common blood], and *selo* [settlement]. It is both a steady look and an enchanted fantasy to imagine the co /*so* petals, the *with* petals, as they do what their parent seed means them to do, means *of* them to do, to detach and become airborne, to disperse and affinitize, to create new orientations. Khlebnikov's linguistic floraculture is but one of several energy units stoking his futurian language-engine; like many of those units it also reflects back onto his exigent world. His projections on language were also dreams of fecundity in a native land of rich soil and chronic famine.

Like molecular armies the word bits make it to the surface, they find vertical or horizontal support. They climb and rise. Or else they burrow down and itch for the mineral attachment. They hum in light, purr in the dark. They make nastic movements, independent of stimulus location. Atop safe carriers they tread the waters. They find the side entrance and evade the larger guards. They clasp the underside. They find release off the cornice. They click and jerk. They sense the host chemical and drop straight down. They bear the strange neighbor, as they are also borne. They move in circles that then move past their own lines. They fuse with cousins. At first glance dull and microbial, as focus and color gain in effect they are revealed to have the spirit of children in a playground. They establish a viable disequilibrium with trellis, lattice, casement. They factor. They crouch in the parallelogram. They enlarge a certain aspect of surface. They sink, become part of slippery bottoms. They hear voices and bells. They twine around dowels, integers of shaded backyard afternoons. They savor excrescence and disarrange symmetries. They infect *and* cauterize. They go toward the quantum fold. They welcome all singularities into the grid. They un-mesh and quiver at the micro-apocalyptic moment. They become toxic as an alternative to distillation. They have truck with gaily-sparkling chunks. They crease along coordinates yet to be made clear. They go outside, they ride on speckled winds. They worry the address with gnat-like interference. They tighten at modulation's first brush. In murk lit by angled setting suns they are part of the swaying world the eye sees against submerged pilings. They grasp at nutrients. They contract to pour motion. They inhere recklessly, like hugging a curve. Their labors are skittish but finally adhesive. They form colander-like catches, they send tendrils out into the abyss. They get THERE on spring-loaded limbs. They singe for warmth. They sidle over to the challenge.

They reduce *and* over-code. They enter with recently-extruded keys.

The across-distance calls of the word bits dripped with light and fluids. Light deliquesced in fluid's excess, imparting to the surroundings the surprise of marine currents. The unrecognizable instar of each word bit began to raise its voice to the animistic possibilities of song. Sometimes a voice detached from its body. It recognized itself in the water's sound on the tiled roof while its body became harder as it freed itself from lunar subtleties. The bits closer to the front slowly opened and straightened their mouths as if fighting against resistance, with small laminations given them by the sweat of caresses. Some bits were determined to resist daylit power-tactics, and fashioned a delicate ceremonial sling. They took up their newborn and stole to the other side of the river. These bits sounded like a tweezer closing. A lyre pointed and stretched its throat toward the whirlwind of the eastern gate. The bits paused, they heard within the exception-to-the-law a whirlwind being devoured by the tides, and felt a pianistic premonition. Efforts to reach the rippling seeds lent them new reflections. All caves turned out, all forests grew field. Rushing clouds banged against a tree and acquired its fleshy verticality, and by way of a crown of leaves, released the fortune of future figurations. A raptor on a calcite crag managed to cross one wing over another, watching the scene below with indifference; it had long known that a shout reproduces itself by the conjugation of click and bump. It came closer, it lit on a tree which cast its shadows upward. One of the bits had grown an appendage that penetrates on the right and emerges on the left. Rainshape, Cloudshape, Woodshape, time spreadeagled and ripe for fucking. With a few strokes the likeness was done and put up for others to judge. All survived their amatory encounters; otherwise the shadows would've died as well, before their chance to mount the room with their slope of groans. A word bit ran through the mirror but emerged before its image did, getting entangled in the double column. This bit grew erect in a particular speck of time, before homogeneity could destroy it. A prior visitation had rubbed it with ashes; a word bit displaying the muscular force of a serpent tried to lick it free. Lust had overcome the players, weaving figures in a grotto. Perhaps the body is thus realized, as windows in a structure blown away and resettling themselves at cardinal points. String games dangled from the sills; syllables crackled in the gold-like spirals gathering in the corner of an eye. Phrases formed intricate systems of such ungraspable causality that only the dying sparks of a

Hyperborean blaze could be perceived. With fresh hands a child seemed to push away a branch, toward a flat surface which held the white that accepts all colors. In doing so, a spectral station was recovered and discovered simultaneously. He looked at that glassy surface and left the sentence incomplete. Walls came undone in eleventh-hour shallowly-breathed promises. Silent, becoming excited by an episodic night's thick water, a word bit edged over the rim of the child's gaze. The door into his heart was breached; fascination sank to an optimal level and arranged a buoyant health. Light was now coming off the skin of the changeling; it had an intensity made all the more stark by a translucent porosity. Word bits heard the reverb switching around the room like exposed wires; they felt the discharge when a fiercely new but long-lost sibling left tooth, tongue, and roof of mouth. Moisture gathered at the edge of the estate. Gravid sounds circled the structure. Thus, as if a spring had been born at the bottom of the ocean, or a drop of water seduced into the middle of a quartz crystal, these bits emboldened, they adhered and entered. The instar could then wait in peaceful torpor as the stripling years beckoned, in waves of pre-breath and ultra-chaos, and all plans for expression became birthmarks in the snow.

■

When I was a kid my want list during the holidays had a single item on it, a "box game." That was as much detail as I wanted to give. It didn't matter what the game was, I never played that. I played the box and the contents. This could take many forms—spreading the pieces out on a table, sequencing them, quadrangling them, animating some of them, setting them at war with one another, turning them into currencies. Pieces representing players still maintained that privileged status, in fact their "agency" was all the more enhanced off the circumscribed pathways of the playing board. This latter was the dullest thing in the box, unless its pastedown regularity was enlivened with slots, movable parts, plastic toggles, and the like. Thinking about this now, I see that I was conflating two conceptual "boxes," each with its own procedural modalities—the game and the kit. The game which is played exchanged edges with the kit which is built, and became the built game. Something with rules crossed borders with something with instructions and, both disregarded, became a cavalier prescriptive space.

But the larger reason for wanting a "box game" wasn't something I could communicate and have it come out right. It was the storage dynamic, which in almost every case trumped the game itself, and my own appropriations. Those *cardboard levels*—up center to hold a spinning wheel (except the level didn't hold it, the wheel simply rested there), levels on either side of the center one (levels of different heights!) to hold play money or directions, with multiple levels below these made from one ingeniously scored piece of cardboard. The playing pieces, so bright and shiny, lay in their niches, calm matte quadrangles of gray or brown. And the whole thing calibrated to leave a clearance of a quarter inch at the top of the box, so the folded playing board could cover its dominion. The afternoon's play might even consist of a cyclical dismantling and replacing: taking each piece out of the box, then the cardboard levels, on down until the box was empty. Then a careful re-assemblage: the levels, the pieces, the playing board, even the lid of the box, and the whole cycle possibly repeated, and then again. My care with these games might have struck a parent as "nice," but the spirit behind it wasn't nicey-nice but fascination. A little more of the "shop" gene showing and it might have been vacuum cleaner motors I took apart and put back together.

This was solitary kit-playing. I would join someone else's play, and invite others to join mine—if we were outdoors. But the time with a box game was a special kind of time, a gap in the "social work" with playmates and even a gap in having fun, if fun implies release. There was the cycle of taking and putting back, but steady attention throughout. (I was ready for fun *afterward*.) This attention didn't have a name and its object didn't have one either. If I wanted to try it in the present, I might be thinking of that crisp word from adulthood, structure, and my activities with plastic pieces and cardboard levels akin to looking that word up.

Whatever it was, it was not repetitive "behavior." The import shifted each time. What's missing here that might have been there with the vacuum cleaner motor was "how things work." With my games it was "how things go together" or "how things are together," a quick step to "how things are." *Are* was intensive. I never believed that the pieces and levels were banished units once the box top closed over them. Their aspect was simply different. Even under cardboard covers they were capable of sharing newly-darkened frequencies with a youngster.

These memory-boxes, each packed with its own afternoons, share space with a single afternoon the memory of which is so bare of even webs and wisps that only my continuing acquaintance with it precludes the possibility of it having been a dream. Even calling it fragmentary is going too far. We are visiting an elderly relative in St. Louis, years before moving there ourselves. It is summer, and I am given a box (small, black) and sat in a side courtyard, a small corridor of outdoor space between this house and the next. (But where is Barbara?) The grown-ups are off doing something else, talking in a living room. The sun-struck corridor where I've been put is made of red brick. (Older neighborhoods in St. Louis are positive *realms* of this material.) It can't be high summer; it would be like throwing Hansel in the oven to put a youngster outside in a cul-de-sac like that. As it is, it's pleasant, and I am always fine alone. When I take the lid off the box, I see rows of small glass bottles, stoppered, each bottle halfway down a slotted hole. (Another cardboard level.) The bottles are maybe two inches tall, straight cylinders, and slightly wider than a pencil. In each bottle is...something. Here the filament is in danger of burning through. Were they slips of paper? Homespun wisdom on them, mass-printed? Were they small minerals or crystals? Maybe even cedar twigs? Was the box sold as such? Or did you buy it empty and turn it into your own compendium?

I believe they were slips of paper with printing on them.

It was a sort of reliquary, with value felt if the vials' contents were opened and scrutinized, but greater value felt if the whole was present and undisturbed, a fetish-communion.

A unit composed of units. Interest signaling among the aggregates.

I do know I didn't un-stopper every bottle. The facts and homilies in the bottles surely tantalized, but so did a vibration of the system, the array as information.

Whenever one comes across useful things, handles them, moves them around, or out of the way, a region has already been discovered. Heidegger is probably thinking of things both humbler and nobler with which to find a region than kids' indoor games from 1960s America. But regions were exactly what opened up, and not from any perception of usefulness. (Odd—sly—that things are already useful before his "one" has even come across them.) Especially in my material subversion of the box games, there was perhaps the first feeling of extension that had a thrill inside it, thrill and captaincy. What seemed useful were the budding regions themselves, the impulsive projections. Giving a little to Heidegger's "useful," it also had a character of recognition.

Bringing these things up makes me remember a poem of mine from years ago, before I'd turned a page of MH. Re-reading it from the magazine it was in, I see that my current paragraph is a variation on a thought-passage previously sounded. It was called "Things You Will Need," a phrase appearing in kids' activity books. "Remember in kindergarten," it asked, "when something// would fly into your head/ from a window, wherever// you didn't know where/ it came from,// but from then on/ it was you?" I was remembering kindergarten moments when I had felt a strange addition settle inside, an addition that could also be described as level, dimension, layer, "when you would deepen/ mysteriously." Without seeming to desire it I felt new beam-paths to "the exterior," paths that expanded interiority as well. Precisely because it wasn't tied in to the terminus of desires denied or fulfilled, but was nonetheless clearly acting in your life, it led outward. "It was something/ away, and older,// coming to join you/ to your remainder." Or, world-entrance as best-case scenario (or at least good), rather than a warp toward accommodation.

"It lived with paste,/ but also with the hair// of strangers." Kindergartners today are surely using a more sophisticated sticker to-er than the gloppy stuff we used, which seemed to come only in vat sizes. It had the color and consistency of cream of wheat and a fairly nice odor (in fact wasn't it called wheat paste?) and was applied to construction paper with a unit that distorted memory says was the size of an umpire's brush. "The hair of strangers" was one particular classmate, identity now lost, seen from behind. It might have lasted no longer than a half minute, but her hair had a facticity—or represented a facticity—that held me in a kind of place. (That placed me in a kind of hold.) More importantly, it was a beholding that seemed to augur a shift, from a child's myopic gaze to a youngster's steady look. I could imagine that hair, that person, that moment, that beholder, *going somewhere*—not literally, but lasting past its half minute, creating stores of implication, factoring even more in. A few days later (or was it a few weeks?) I had a chat with a different girl, a frizzy-haired miniature named Iva Blagg, and surely the first conversation ever with someone not in my immediate family, and maybe not even them. The conversation consisted of one fib after another tossed back and forth between us, about all the snakes we'd encountered in our lives.

The envelope-pushing manipulator of box games is three or four years older than that other self lying about snakes, and in the intervening period the stores of implication have grown. He has become something of a knowing androgyne, letting the power-magic of others seep across the threshold. (Willing it across might be more accurate.) And though the power-magic belongs to things as well as others, it is the other's carnal body, the happened-upon blunt wonder at the bend in the garden, that is the sovereign occupant of the new land. In *Les Enfants Terribles,* Cocteau had shown us Dargelos, the snowball-throwing brute whose beauty and cunning had conferred upon him a schoolyard version of the divine right of kings, making him almost a peer of the grown-ups (who in turn had become, reluctantly or not, near-accomplices). But the same character in Cocteau's film *Le Sang d'un Poète* has another clearer aspect, which may or may not have belonged to the boy in the novel. In the film, Dargelos is a character but also a type. He is *the bigger boy*—the one in short pants and sailor's cap like the others, but with a precocious weight and height that makes him a creature of fascination. Never book-smart, he often falls into the bully role. He inspires fear in the other boys, but also exploratory heat. He is the herald of adult bodies (those knees! that shoulder span!) and the exotic and exciting country they live in.

Exotic, but as close as a breath.

> *June 22. Fresh on the bus, I walk to the rear and the empty seats. There's one next to a guy with tattoos and one opposite, which I take because I want to have a better view. Tats cover him. They're artfully spaced apart but they're all over. The fact that he's clean-shaven and short-haired almost gives another level of interest to the whole. His shorts are short and his tee is tight so there's a lot to notice. They're not "grunge" tats, they're sprightly, well-drawn, even a little goofy. And the spacing also sets them apart. The tats signify "graphic design" rather than, say, "subculture." Curvature and sitting position disallowed a clear sense of most of the designs but his left thigh was covered with a checkered box that had a spiral coming out of it. Whether it was meant to be an actual spiral or a representation of spiral motion I don't know. The checks were in alternating orange and black in square half-inches with strong black borders (or was it black alternating with his untatted flesh tone?) It's a sunny day so I'm wearing shades and can see with some circumspection the integrity that this particular passenger gives to skin art—skin as canvas, skin as body,*

skin as displayed social body. Tats are ubiquitous in San Francisco but his were something special, eye-capturing, bold as it gets but in no way harsh. If I myself were bolder I'd have gotten off at his stop. I'd have wanted to ask, what else is in the box.

"It became a sort of project// that followed you/ on rounds."

Other-fascination and a growing trespass into times and distances. A djinn, a floating tag. The faux-metaphysical current that melds into the structures of a project. Neighborhoods and their treetops start to build the incline. It does follow me on rounds; it is the rounds.

Once sounded never stopped. Pushed out of doors, pushed into a room. Encompassing movements. The rope communicating hold, "I" in single-file. The project is a minutely-perforated advance/expanse.

I want to go into spaces, their implications.

■

"I like the bigness of things, their largeness." The opening sentence of Bruce Boone's *Century of Clouds* is my favorite opening of any work. Such a subtle unconventionality, that floating end-phrase, subtle and radical. "Their largeness" makes conclusive a prior phrase and also sets itself up to roam free. From that period we venture out.

In the present moment I am writing on what used to be the back of a sack. I still buy CDs, and accumulate plenty of slip-in, bottomless paper sacks. A quick swish with a letter opener and I have two sheets of writing paper. At some point a bunch of these get stuffed into a clipboard. Poor methodology, but nice messy vibrations. I have to sort through, shuffle, search both sides of a sheet, and/or turn a sheet upside down to use the space left over from an earlier day's paragraph. The next day the active sheet is somewhere inside, never on top. The rummage process picks up again.

This sloppy method exists for more than one reason but most of them have to do with finding the oblique territory, the one that will allow me a tenuous border with, and so possible crossover to, the matter at hand, a large but piecemeal locality. (Some of the lights of this locality show clearly while others are under straw.

On a different day they will have exchanged their intensities.) Working through to an exigent matter at hand seems to require this slightly tricked-up, rough-hewn procedure. It requires my own visceral participation in makeshift arrangements, my occupancy as passenger on a scrap.

When Tony Smith was teaching art at Cooper Union in the early 50s, "someone told me how I could get onto the unfinished New Jersey Turnpike. I took three students and drove from somewhere in the Meadows to New Brunswick. It was a dark night and there were no lights or shoulder markers, lines, railings, or anything at all except the dark pavement moving through the landscape of the flats, rimmed by hills in the distance, but punctuated by stacks, towers, fumes, and colored lights." By a serendipitous opportunity, four people experienced not the promise of the open road but the novelty of a road made more thrillingly open by virtue of not being ready. Emptied of ordinary instrumentality, the experience filled with panpsychic possibilities, speed and speculation, a past-less thrust. And forming a template along with the momentum, the rough tracing of aesthetic. Whitehead's "lure for feeling" tractioning toward a project.

A modest house on the outskirts of Du Quoin, probably built in the 1920s, where I lived with my brother and a few of his friends for half a year. Shabby furniture, dusty drapes. A main room. ("Living room" is too grand.) An upstairs, two tiny attic-like rooms to the left and right of the staircase. Two original bedrooms downstairs and a third, a tack-on, past the bathroom.

■

A house in the center of town, next to the First Christian Church on Main, which we called "the white house." Once a house people lived in like any other, it was now an adjunct to the church. Former bedrooms were sort-of offices, but mostly unused. The large living room had a desk at one end and a sofa and chairs at the other for meetings. Downstairs was a concrete-floored, bare-bulb "rec" area. And past the stairs on the main level was the minister's office, the only truly serious place in the building. Its door was always open but the room felt off-limits, even to us teenagers who came to the house any time and stayed endlessly.

■

The basement of a neighbor's house, next to ours on Laurel Avenue, a small play space, the steps to the basement linoleum-covered planks with no railing.

These are the spaces that won't let me go. I live stretches of my life that seem to be transpiring in the given locality, only to become conscious of an expanded space—a kind of psycho-sensory fog lift—that reveals the "past life" circumferent ambience of one of these three. Benign but unsought, they somehow managed to slip past "the clearing house" and have set up shop. Not constant, and in no way important, they are nevertheless impervious to the blessings of mnemonic decay. One or two other spaces make brief appearances but these three are the mainstays. There have been no additions to these rooms and buildings from the last thirty-five years; all are from living situations earlier in life, and not terribly consequential even then. The last one, the neighbor's basement, is a real puzzle, since I couldn't have been down there more than four or five times.

It's not that scenes from things I read float to these sites and transpire there. I don't imagine myself doing whatever I do in them. But in their diaphanous way they encircle the local space, the room I'm in even when I'm outdoors. Like anxiety, they are everywhere and nowhere. They never make a demand; they never make a sound. I must shift to waking life to notice that they have been there.

In getting toward a poem-thing, it may be that I'm trying to call out some site that has this double character, of distance and persistence. But what I'm trying to get toward is a site without precedence, one part faint and nine parts persistent, and the task is to find "the mortal line of equilibrium." Or *not*: the task may seem to make the lesser and greater parts speak to each other while maintaining the discrepancy.

Site: an overused word in words on poetry. But apt in one way. The site is the *in potentia,* where the momentous and the momentary can exchange signals. In poetry, though, when the poem has happened, the site remains.

In Moroccan Arabic there is a root, *rsm.* Stefania Pandolfo says it means "to fix and to settle, to immobilize, to orient, to establish; but also to draw, to describe, to inscribe, to fix in images." It thus can set something in place (building) and get something down (sketching, writing). Homes in the Dra[c] valley are vulnerable—

to the elements, to the occasional enemy. Vulnerability such as this accelerates the cycle, and the stresses, of ending and beginning. The terms for building are never far from their opposites, are never far from day-to-day consciousness. If a house can be a *rasm,* it can also be subject to *sheṭṭeb,* clearing out, erasing. The sequence is blurred by the accelerated cycle; erasure has the added shading of preparation. In a village of attritional loss and incremental gain, reclamation can be a spirit that rises above the actual. The main tradition of oral poetry in the territory is called *rasma.* Its coming from *rsm* is an only slightly more emphatic lineage than terms from Arabic poetry at large, where "a stanza is a *bît* (classical *al-bait*), a term that means 'house,' 'building,' and in vernacular 'room,' and that carries in both classical and vernacular the poetic meaning of 'verse.'" In the valley, the proximity of poetry-making to building is necessarily intensified. The following term meaning to describe or fix in place can be adopted by a poet and made to speak his own construction: "kan-rassem," *I compose.*

> *June 2. Coming back home after a week in Seattle, I was struck by how regulated the space in San Francisco is. In Seattle I could easily imagine "setting myself up" as an afternoon book-reader, say, by "setting myself*

down" virtually anywhere. I could imagine, for example, walking a few blocks from Pioneer Square down to the bay, turning down one of the low-foot-traffic, old-warehouse streets, or under the freeway, and finding on the pavement a crate or even still-usable chair to sit on, there or elsewhere, and open my book or otherwise get to work. I feel like I could have dragged this imaginary chair back to Pioneer Square, and opened a book or notebook, or just took things in, and it would not have created a detectable flap in any texture. If I tried to do this in San Francisco, I would be "questioned." But Seattle felt otherwise, it still possessed unaccounted space.

Once there was a vivid daydream and I wrote a poem-paragraph describing it. A "tribe" spent their lives swimming under polar ice, looking for air pockets. The air pockets were sought for rest and breathing, but those were secondary concerns. The real purpose was so that the tribe members could scan the walls of ice they were temporarily under. Picture-messages would appear on the pocket-walls that told them what had to be done next. One message mentioned an image of a red schoolhouse, perhaps a mnemonic for the tribe, of right-angled, scripted instruction, of learning as security, growth in the enclosure.

Part of the pull of the wonder-cabinet is to have you inside it, dreaming worlds along with the shells and beetles. The infinite is also a hut.

Morton Feldman wrote on his walls. "I put sheets of graph paper on the wall; each sheet framed the same time duration and was, in effect, a visual rhythmic structure." Schoenberg could do it without the paper, he could *see* the structure of the piece he wanted to write, a cat's-cradle hovering in the room. Faulkner lined his walls with chapter outlines; the outlines of the book he was working on when he was thrown by the horse are still up. Nettie Young, one of the quilters of Gee's Bend, could get an idea for a quilt design by studying make-do insulation. "You'd gather paper and plaster it on your walls. That's all you had on your wall. You'd see any kind of old book, any kind of old newspaper—you'd plaster the wall, to keep the wind from coming in your home. And then sometimes you'd be sitting down looking at your wall, and you'll *see* something—on that paper, take your attention. And you'll think *that's something good, I could do something with this*. And you put it together in your head. And you do it."

Sites of the transient, except huts can go all the way down to the other side. If not for bad dreams, Hamlet could be "bounded in a nutshell and count myself king of infinite space." In *The Hamlet,* a field hand leads a cow, his lover, across woods and pastures in a blazing high noon that gathers the arc of the earth and condenses it into a driven structure in his head. Every freely gained foot of walked space only tightens the interior. What put *that* in your nut? a character in a play asks his brother. A musician working with Arthur Russell in the studio remembered him as someone "addicted to his caves—the caves of his mind and the caves he lived in. He had a dark, hidden, cubbyhole quality to his thinking." A lot of poets live in their heads, and some dream of the small space that could draw that life-form out, and externalize it, and leave them merely alert.

Ann Cline built a tea hut in her back yard. She left some spaces in the walls to look out— windows is saying it too strongly. She noticed that the spaces nearest the floor "brought me the most pleasure: by extending the floor to the surrounding ground, nearby tree trunks and falling leaves, unremarkable in full view, became passionate vignettes." A sukkah, a hut or booth built to observe the Jewish harvest: an echo of shelter in the wilderness. In keeping with the reverberant necessities of those in flight, the roof of a sukkah can't be made of anything functional. Twigs and branches therefore bloom to use, as they serve another standard, that the roof be made of things once but no longer attached to the earth. It was surely from roofs made in this way that a further requirement evolved for the commemorative sukkah, one that melds the spindliness of the hastily-made wildernesss sukkah into opportunities for teleological reflection: at night, you must be able to see stars through the roof.

Small space is totality's diagram, considered in a respite from totality's interference. But the best small space has slivers of interference. The sliver could be the gap that reveals "passionate vignettes," or a glint of consciousness. The person who feels the requirement, or goes to the trouble, of making these arrangements, is somewhere near *Being and Time*'s "self-directive discovering of a region...grounded in an ecstatically retentive awaiting of the possible hither and whither." *Near* is the classic Heideggerian place, where hints and auspices are within reach, awaiting use, or deferral. The Near is the house of tools. But for some, what's being built with it may be less a region than an inflection, a thought-whisper. Vulnerability, which is a form of receptivity, is in the building instructions. Just as huts with their tolerance for the idiosyncratic are a form of infinity. In The Book of Tea, Okakura describes a tea hut: an ephemeral structure built to house a poetic impulse. Kamo no

Chomei, living in poverty amid shifting dynasties, goes further in something mentioned by Cline, only in a hut built for the moment can one live without fears.

Space become place inside a blanket's four corners. We laid the quilt down on the grass just above the lake and slept like rocks. A quilt on grass, a brief and eternal cohesion. The people camping-living in the United Nations Plaza, their lain tarps. Pixie and Dixie house under a ping-pong table, the governing rectangle a "ceiling," the underside of the playing surface. My legal pad's quadrilateral, a boxy encumbrance when nothing's happening but a peering well when something is. The placing of a cloth, the subtle adjustments made, initiating or closing an occasion, or being in the midst of one. The Maghribî, engaged in *l-frâsh,* "putting the rugs down." This means "to materialize for a moment the space of a house, to create a fugitive permanence. Before meaning 'house,' *rasm* means 'tent.' For open-air ritual events—the henna ceremony at weddings, for example—"a place is materialized by putting down a straw mat. On that mat—a symbolic rasm—a whole world can be made to appear."

May 9. Getting on the Castro-bound 24, I see immediately that all the seats are taken, and I can only move as far back as the side exit door. Turning back to face the front I notice the standee nearest to me, a fully-grown adult, a very young man. He's short, slight, softly in the world, and hirsute. "Sephardic" is my first unknowing response to his person. He watches the outside's everyday street parade with a kind of studious rapture, a babe in wonderland. Apart from aspects of personality (shy and curious being the first flashes), the most striking thing about him, to me and surely anyone else looking his way, is his ass, enclosed in very tight and short cut-offs, and assertively cocked. It looks like the bottom of the boy standing on the diving rock in Eakins' "The Swimming Hole." The gay signal is loud and clear but so, somehow, is the innocence of its expression. He's announcing, not selling. (If he'd been on the 19 Polk things might have messaged differently.) He seems instead to be celebrating the other side of a threshold, past a teenager's struggles to the place in the sun. In a few years some more experience will have sifted into his adventures and he might then go for a softer, all-around look rather than this tightly-focused one. Meanwhile this one, practiced and brash, is lovely in its way, as I hope the ones to come will also be.

In Greek there is a root, *kti-*. D. F. Krell believes it "comes from the Sanskrit word *kséti,* meaning 'to reside,' and *ksitis,* 'habitation.'" It made its way into Greek in words like "κτίζω, κτίσις, 'settling, founding, creating,' 'creature, creation,' but also 'building,' as in the erection of a temple or sanctuary." But these words come from a Greek root, *tic,* that was the next stepping stone from the Sanskrit. This root is related to creation but principally denotes *pro*creation, engendering, inseminating. *Tic* is sexual love as something that creates. Krell believes that at some point there was a shift from *tic* to *tec,* from love to work, in the ways people thought and spoke about building. Τέχνη, *technique,* becomes the new-rationalist replacement for τίκτω, *to produce.*

Here a term intrudes, settles like a boulder. Bland and general in casual usage, it has a phosphorescent glow in specific placements. It is a quick synonym for selfishness and an obscure but desired object of ontological striving. It is a vacuum, the absence of particulate reality. It is also a blotter inviting all. It's a neutered technical abstraction, and the deepest reach of Eros. This term, "the world," says nothing and everything, depending on the pressure. "Abstraction emerges as necessary to modernism when representations can no longer be the bearer of our conviction and connectedness to the world," J. M. Bernstein writes in *Against Voluptuous Bodies.* "The world opened up for me," Daniel Bell says of his youthful discovery of socialism, in a documentary called *Arguing the World.* This phenomenon was clear to Wilhelm Dilthey, who could tell that "at each instance, understanding discloses a world." Speaking of Leonardo's "Virgin of the Rocks," T. J. Clark can't help noticing the drapery, "the key to Renaissance painting's sense of the body expanding and luxuriating in the world." The lovers in *Nightwood* "were alone and happy, apart from the world in their appreciation of the world." "Da-sein is never 'initially' a sort of a being which is free from being-in, but which at times is in the mood to take up a 'relation' to the world." We want to take those relations up. We want that position. "One evening I'm lying on my bed, the butch one. I'm watching teevee. The bed's next to the window, so I'm looking at the tube but I'm also in the world." Eileen, I put myself there all the time. I love divided consciousness.

Near the end of the "Ktaadn" section of *The Maine Woods,* Thoreau comes as close as he ever will to losing himself, at least in print. Throughout the *Woods* he is the person I think I know, the temperate close observer, keeping his own counsel and even challenging his Penobscot guide on the best ways to manage the outdoors. The writing is his familiar wood and flint, with its proto-objectivist aim of letting the situation rematerialize from a complex of clear observations. But after an experience seemingly no different in intensity from others around it, he joins the holy man under the cowl and goes off. "What is it to be admitted to a museum, to see a myriad of particular things, compared with being shown some star's surface, some hard matter in its home! I stand in awe of my body, this matter to which I am bound has become so strange to me. What is this Titan that has possession of me? Talk of mysteries!—Think of our life in nature,—daily to be shown matter, to come in contact with it,—rocks, trees, wind on our cheeks! The *solid* earth! the *actual* world! the *common sense! Contact! Contact! Who* are we? *where* are we?"

> I look at my hand in the dawning.
> I look at the veins contained there.
> I look at them in amazement
> as I would look at a stranger.

Manuel Flores, in this poem of Borges, is in the grip of the world-gift: the happily quizzical situation of being present, and in myriad realizations well before or otherwise not conversant with its version in Christianity. It is Hannah Arendt, mentioning "the famous contention of Plato, quoted by Aristotle, that *thaumazein,* the shocked wonder at the miracle of Being, is the beginning of all philosophy." It is also the Kabbalah scholar Moshe Idel, saying "Love of the cosmic cause in relation to its effects and vice versa." It's the sheer stun, against infinitesimal odds, of being one who made it to the surface of life. An arching body, and bread-crumb attentions: advancing the bone-roll of life with peering steps. Self and others: the dance of affect, the comfort of difference. Eros in the round. Harry Partch between microtones, saying: "Mood, sky, and circumstance." *The World and its Streets, Places.* And, with the knowledge of infinitesimal odds, a mirage of infinity. A twentieth-century American poet writes in his daybook "surely infiniteness is the most evident thing in the world."

Forty years after *Being and Time* and its "one" coming across "useful things," this poet wrote "There are things/ We live among 'and to see them/ Is to know ourselves.'" Both Heidegger and George Oppen understand the condition-quality of conscious life. They also share awareness of emergent conditions. But temperaments, and pronouns, create divergent empathic worlds. Heidegger's discovery of a region is quickened by things the individual-in-progress comes across, in a narratively powerful section about disclosed potential. Oppen's opening-out narrative is contingent on human relations long considered, on acknowledgment, on tasks *after* discovery. (*The Materials:* both starting with *and* having decided on.) Heidegger's single consciousness will have lived past its cut-off point in *Being and Time* before encountering Oppen's "shipwreck of the singular," the knowledge of ultimate aloneness which has nevertheless chosen to live in "the meaning/ of being numerous." A noble choice, a resigned choice: the deepest breaths coming inside the antinomies. The infiniteness is most evident when seen in "the bright light/ of shipwreck," the disruptively luminous fact-event-discovery that sharpens its recipient and ultimately sets her direction, however reluctantly taken up, toward the social. Heidegger's finding, Oppen's seeing: related inquiries, irregular stresses. For the former, accretions along the forest path that fulfill the human project as a form of self-sovereignty; for the latter, a casting off into waters that may or may not get you to a safer place, but worth the risk all the same, "for the sake of an instant in the eyes."

■

Pandolfo's Maghribî are being moved. They are being moved from the "qṣar"—a word meaning palace but applied by the Maghribî to the walled settlement that has been their home, their idea of home, since most of their memories started. They are moving from the qṣar's congested memory-maze to a modernized copy of the same, the new village, meant to duplicate the plan of the qṣar but without the impacted proximities to everything else that, along with the occasional falling wall, made trials of daily life. And yet, even with close collaboration with the builders and a no-interference policy from the agency putting up the money, nothing is quite right in the new village. (Nothing *quite* right: the power to unnerve.) The walls bear better, but cradle nothing. "People suddenly realized," Pandolfo wrote, "that in the New Village the old neighbors were not neighbors anymore." For the oldest among them, the experience has been not simply a move from one place to another but the breaking of ontological foundations. An internalized spatiality, a spatiality of the soul, must now look at a suddenly stronger sun, a sun that feels like wattage. The new interior spaces are better lit but that is saying they are no longer *modeled* with light. The mud-walled homes of the qṣar, vulnerable to time and sudden storms, were affective presences, familiars made from the elements. Their absence is not compensated for by durability. The old staircases were particularly resonant, they were part of time. Their disappearance is acutely felt. They had been "embedded in the internal structure of the building. Invisible, dynamic, and alive, they cannot be seen from the outside, or from inside the downstairs room. Narrow and dark, they withdraw from sight even as one climbs their winding steps; one is carried up by their movement as if blind." To climb a staircase such as this was an everyday household occurrence, but the inhabitant also engaged in a complex of action involving upward motion, sightlessness, and faith. It was assurance not from but in the dark. Even the foundation of the staircase was protection from a further "under." "Masons call this base *aferdu,* after the compact wooden base of the mortar and by analogy with the Iferd, a mythical pond of rotting water in communication with the realm of death and the Below. The work of the staircase is a process of displacement of that base of oblivion, which is spun and woven into an elevated, articulated structure." Elevate and articulate: descriptions that, shorn of their past participles, become measures of belief.

Can interior rising such as this, transplanted to other places, other situations, also be "corridors of power"? What was a daily experience with many of the Maghribî has been a rare one for myself. In my experience only a few literal ascendances have been charged with meaning. There was the natural rock passage I squeezed through to a higher elevation with friends in a state park. But there was also the pair of right-angle turns leading to the stairways that take you up, up, to the transcendental main room in Wright's Unity Temple in Chicago's Oak Park suburb. Those two hard right-angle turns into, through, and out of a dark vestibule, are, in Philip Johnson's words, a "wrench." They were actions that linked you to a processional awareness that some of the most meaningful choices in life will be passionately abrupt.

Today in the world and its pleats, graces, I have a somewhere-feeling. It's kitty-corner from the block I'm on, actually kitty-corner two blocks away, a double-diagonal. I'm certain that's where it is. There's a raw structure on the block, featureless, particular. Other stuff is on the block but this is *really* on it. Two walls are up, attached, and both are joined to a concrete floor. The other two walls, the ones that would complete an enclosure, are not there.

This half cube, were it to become whole, is not a human-scale room. It's large large, anticipating floors of humans. Surely pencil markings or even little ratchets will soon materialize on the walls, showing where the floor/ceilings will go. Or else it's small small, a budding object or contraption, awaiting the return of the builder or first impressions of the beholder. Invisible valences and rushing occasions make it oscillate between large and small. Either way, this structure and I seem to have an impression of each other. In thinking about it, or even just knowing news of it, I'm as-good-as visiting it, even as it in turn has made the most direct overtures, even four blocks away, or is it two.

I know the overtures are direct because they reach me, as bits of sound from close and distant work. (Bits of sound = bits of use.) Scraping, attaching, priming. But the structure stays in place. Or on rare occasions a seismic boom meets it with a single subterranean POW, and birds that had paused atop one of the sides clear off, to fly in my direction. Not songbirds but animals of the air like rocs, bringing and shedding heavier, more consequential bits of sound. But is it really sound? Isn't it more like the wave-impact just prior to sound? A calibration, a pinprick through which, tele-micro-scoping my squint, an inquiry might be made out? "I've got you right where you want me," the lover's stratagem? All I know is at that point I can press the event and be something of a joiner, having become a near-involuntary correspondent to this beckoning, even nagging, perplex—of desire and the mirage, of a hard demand in concert with suspended rustling, soft enough to set me into my questions but obviously sturdy enough to let these animals rest at the top before they fly off again. They had to come from that direction. Because, as I said, I'm almost certain that was it.

The following works came into play, some of them short but sweet, during the writing of *Aspiration:* Hannah Arendt, *The Human Condition* (University of Chicago Press, 1958); Hugo Ball, *Flight Out of Time: A Dada Diary,* edited by John Elderfield (University of California Press, 1996); Djuna Barnes, *Nightwood* (New Directions, 1946); J. M. Bernstein, *Against Voluptuous Bodies: Late Modernism and the Meaning of Painting* (Stanford University Press, 2006); Bruce Boone, *Century of Clouds* (Nightboat Books, 2009); Jorge Luis Borges, *Selected Poems,* edited by Alexander Coleman (Viking Press, 1999); John Cage, "Empty Words with Relevant Material," from *Talking Poetics from Naropa Institute: Annals of the Jack Kerouac School of Disembodied Poetics, Volume One* (Shambhala, 1978); T. J. Clark, "The Chill of Disillusion," in *The London Review of Books* (January 5, 2012), pp. 6-7; Ann Cline, *A Hut of One's Own: Life Outside the Circle of Architecture* (MIT Press, 1997); Henry Corbin, *Alone With the Alone: Creative Imagination in the Sūfism of Ibn ʿArabī,* translated by Ralph Manheim (Princeton University Press, 1969); Don DeLillo, *Ratner's Star* (Knopf, 1976); Dorothea Dietrich, Brigid Doherty, Sabine Kriebel, and Leah Dickerman, *Dada: Zurich, Berlin, Hannover, Cologne, New York, Paris* (National Gallery of Art, Washington/D.A.P., 2008); Morton Feldman, *Give My Regards to Eighth Street* (Exact Change, 2004); Michael Fried, "Art and Objecthood," in *Minimal Art: A Critical Anthology,* edited by Gregory Battcock (Dutton, 1968); Martin Heidegger, *Being and Time,* translated by Joan

Stambaugh, revised by Dennis J. Schmidt (State University of New York Press, 2010); Moshe Idel, *Kabbalah & Eros* (Yale University Press, 2005); David Farrell Krell, *Archeticture* [sic]: *Ecstasies of Space, Time, and the Human Body* (State University of New York Press, 1997); Tim Lawrence, *Hold On To Your Dreams: Arthur Russell and the Downtown Music Scene, 1973-1992* (Duke University Press, 2009); Louis Massignon, "The Idea of the Spirit in Islam," translated by Ralph Manheim, in *The Mystic Vision: Papers from the Eranos Yearbooks,* edited by Joseph Campbell (Princeton University Press, 1983); G. R. S. Mead, *Echoes from the Gnosis* (Quest Books, 2006); Robert Motherwell, *The Dada Painters and Poets: An Anthology, Second Edition* (Belknap Press of Harvard University Press, 1989); Eileen Myles, *Inferno: (A Poet's Novel),* (OR Press, 2010); Frank O'Hara, *The Collected Poems of Frank O'Hara,* edited by Donald Allen (Knopf, 1971); George Oppen, *New Collected Poems,* edited by Michael Davidson (New Directions, 2002); Stefania Pandolfo, *Impasse of the Angels: Scenes from a Moroccan Space of Memory* (University of Chicago Press, 1997); Jerome Rothenberg and Pierre Joris, *Poems for the Millennium, Volume 1: from Fin-de-Siècle to Negritude* (University of California Press, 1995); and Henry D. Thoreau, *The Maine Woods,* edited by Joseph J. Moldenhauer (Princeton University Press, 1972).

Velimir Khlebnikov's "Here is the way the syllable *so* is a field," "On the Simple Names of Language," and "A Checklist: The Alphabet of the Mind," appear in *The Collected Works of Velimir Khlebnikov, Volume I: Letters and Theoretical Writings,* translated by Paul Schmidt (Harvard University Press, 1987).

The diagram is Khlebnikov's own, with my addition of the roman-character transliteration and English equivalents.

"The lyric is..." borrows, in addition to the Pandolfo, Fried, and Heidegger texts cited above, words from Eve Kosofsky Sedgwick, Ermanno Bencivenga, Robert Venturi, Jesse Reiser and Nanako Umemoto, and especially Stephen Shaviro's *Without Criteria: Kant, Whitehead, Deleuze, and Aesthetics* (MIT Press, 2009), both Shaviro's own words and people he quotes: Whitehead, Gilles Deleuze, Gilbert Simondon, and Alberto Toscano.

The strange paragraph beginning "The across-distance calls of the word bits..." is an act of vocabulary and syntactic plunder from the even-stranger "manatee" section of José Lezama Lima's *Paradiso,* translated by Gregory Rabassa (revised edition, Dalkey Archive, 2000), 48-51.

Nettie Jones speaks to us from Vanessa Vadim's 2002 film, *Quilts of Gee's Bend.*

George Albon is the author of *Empire Life* (Littoral Books), *Thousands Count Out Loud* (lyric & press), *Brief Capital of Disturbances* (Omnidawn), *Step* (Post-Apollo), and *Momentary Songs* (Krupskaya). His work has appeared in *Hambone, New American Writing, O Anthology 4, Avec Sampler 1,* and the anthologies *The Gertrude Stein Awards in Innovative American Poetry, Bay Poetics,* and *Blood and Tears: Poems for Matthew Shepard.* His essay "The Paradise of Meaning" was the George Oppen Memorial Lecture for 2002. He lives and works in San Francisco.